Fish

Deirdre McQuillan

ILLUSTRATED BY ALWYN GILLESPIE

Putnam

G.P. Putnam's Sons
Publishers Since 1838
200 Madison Avenue
New York, NY 10016

First American Edition 1992

Library of Congress Cataloging-in-Publication Data

McQuillan, Deirdre

Perfectly simple fish/Deirdre McQuillan;
illustrated by Alwyn Gillespie — 1st American ed.
p.   cm.

ISBN 0-399-13784-X

1. Cookery (Pasta)

Printed in the E.C.
1 2 3 4 5 6 7 8 9 10

Introduction

"God made food, the devil the cooks," wrote James Joyce in Ulysses. Many people are put off from cooking fish by penitential memories of boiled haddock or fried whiting. Yet the pleasure of eating a freshly-caught wild salmon, the briny taste of an oyster, the aroma of a trout grilling over an open fire are the stuff of music, poetry and song. Fish, rich in vitamins, minerals, and protein, is the least spoiled of all our foods, yet it is the one that goes bad the fastest. The secret of culinary success is always to insist on the freshest fish in season. And never overcook it. The great surprise in store for the amateur is how fast the whole procedure can be. Then there are all the varieties – and it's worth going to a fish market just to see them – many of which never reach the stores.

In *North Atlantic Seafood* Alan Davidson lists nearly 200 species of edible fish in the vast realms of that ocean. These days luxury fish are globetrotters that travel first class to satisfy the gourmet palate. I've seen farmed sea bass from America on sale in Dublin; fish farming is only in its infancy.

The recipes in this book are mostly simple and elementary, but their techniques can be applied to many types of fish and may inspire an enthusiast to trawl further afield. In the meantime, get hooked on a good fish market, learn how to look a fresh fish straight in the eye and get off to a frying start!

Basic Fish Stock

This is simple to make and can be frozen (like ice cubes and then bagged) for use when needed. It is the basis for many soups, pies and sauces. Some experts say that sole and flounder make the best stock, but ask your fish market for a selection of fish.

2–3 lb of fish bones, trimmings, heads and skin
1 whole onion, sliced
1 carrot, chopped
1 stalk of celery, chopped
1 tbsp wine vinegar
1 wine glass white wine
1–1½ cups cold water
10 whole peppercorns
bouquet garni

Wash off any remaining blood on the fish under a tap. In a large pot, place in the cold water and the fish pieces, bring to a boil, skimming occasionally. Now add the rest of the ingredients, cover, and allow to simmer for 30 minutes. Strain, return strained liquid to the pot, and leave at full boil for about 15 minutes to reduce stock by about ⅓. Do not add salt. When cool, stock can be frozen and kept until needed.

Fish Soup

A rich, colorful and nutritious soup that is a meal in itself. It can be frozen successfully, and, if you wish, you can leave out the mussels.

2 tbsp butter
3 carrots, sliced
2 sticks celery, chopped
1 leek, cleaned and chopped
5 snow peas, chopped
1 lb potatoes chopped in ¹/₂ inch cubes
³/₄ pt fish stock
1 wine glass white wine
3 tbsp cream
1 lb cod fillets, cut into chunks
12 scrubbed and bearded mussels
salt and pepper
chopped parsley

Melt butter in a pot and soften the vegetables (not the potatoes) for about 5 minutes. Add potatoes and soften in the butter for about 3 minutes. Add fish stock, white wine, and cream, bring to a boil and simmer until potatoes are cooked, about 15–20 minutes. Now add the cod and simmer for about 3 minutes. Then add mussels, cover, and simmer for another 2–3 minutes. Season with salt and pepper, stir in chopped parsley and serve in a warmed tureen with chunks of fresh white bread.

Smokies

A perfect start to a dinner party for 6 – tangy and appetizing – and a breeze to make.

1 medium onion, chopped
¹/₂ stick butter
10oz smoked trout fillets
4 large tomatoes
8oz hard cheese, grated
juice of 1 lemon
¹/₂ tsp sugar
salt and pepper

Preheat oven to 400°F. Peel and chop onions and sweat them in butter until soft and golden. Break up trout into big bite-size pieces. Core the tomatoes and plunge into boiling water for a few minutes, then into cold water and peel off skin, deseed and chop. Grate about 6 ounces of the cheese, retain the rest for sprinkling on top. Mix all the ingredients together in a bowl, add lemon juice, sugar, and season to taste. Divide this mixture into 6 ramekin dishes, sprinkle remaining cheese on top and bake until brown and bubbling for about 15–20 minutes.

Mussel and Potato Salad

A detailed recipe for this dish was once given in a play by Alexandre Dumas, calling for a glass of Château d'Yquem and had instructions for surrounding the dish with truffles cooked in champagne! For some reason, it has often been known as a Japanese salad; either way, it is the most delicious cold (or warm) salad whose success lies in the way in which the warm potatoes absorb the flavors of the wine, the herbs, and vinaigrette.

2 ¼ lb mussels	3 tsp Dijon mustard
4 sprigs parsley	1½ lb potatoes
¼ pt white wine	1 wine glass Noilly Prat
1 stalk celery, chopped	or White Martini
6 peppercorns, crushed	(dry vermouth)
6 tbsp olive oil	1 tbsp thyme, chopped
3 tbsp white wine vinegar	1 tbsp parsley, chopped
(Orleans or tarragon)	2 shallots, chopped

Put the clean, scrubbed, and bearded mussels in a deep pot with white wine, parsley sprigs, celery, and peppercorns. Cover and bring to the boil for a couple of minutes until the mussels open. Remove mussels from their shells and set them aside to cool. Blend the olive oil, wine vinegar, and the mustard in a blender and set aside. Boil the potatoes in the mussel juices and water and when they are cooked, peel quickly while still hot and slice thickly into a large bowl. At the same time, mix in the vermouth and then the chopped fresh herbs including shallots and finally toss in the vinaigrette and the mussels. Serve immediately sprinkled with chopped parsley or leave to chill, covered, in a refrigerator.

Angels on Horseback

Being Irish, I think the best way to eat a host of Galway oysters is *au naturel* with a dash of lemon juice, plenty of buttered brown bread, and Guinness. These old favorites, however, make a party snack or appetizer and are a good introduction to cooked oysters for those who have never tasted them before.

16 oysters shucked (ask the fish
market to do it if you can't)
8 rashers of streaky bacon, cut in half
4 big slices of hot buttered toast
lemon wedges

Preheat broiler. Drain oysters and pat dry. Wind a piece of streaky bacon around each oyster and skewer with a wooden toothpick or cocktail stick. Broil on both sides until the bacon is brown and crispy and serve with the hot buttered toast and lemon wedges.

Crab Pâté

8oz fresh crab meat
1 stick butter, softened
1 shallot, finely chopped
1 tbsp parsley, chopped
1 clove of garlic, crushed
ground pepper
pinch cayenne pepper
lemon juice to taste
2 fl oz fish stock
1 tbsp tomato and zucchini chutney
fresh herbs for garnish, such as chives,
parsley, chervil, chopped

Blend crab meat with butter, shallot, parsley, garlic, cayenne, pepper, lemon juice, fish stock, and chutney in a blender or food processor. Check seasoning to taste. Press the mixture into a bowl, cover, and chill. Alternatively, roll it like a sausage in wax paper, twisting the ends and chill. Before serving, roll it over a bed of chopped fresh herbs, such as chives, parsley, or chervil, to cover. Good with thin slices of hot buttered toast or brown bread and lemon wedges.

Potted Shrimps

Shrimps are known as the fleas or scavengers of the sea and some have the ability to change their color depending on the sand that they are in. Potting shrimps was an old method of preservation that goes back to Tudor times. Undoubtedly, the best potted shrimps are those you make yourself.

1 lb large fresh shrimp
1 shallot, chopped
bay leaf
sprig thyme
1 stalk of celery, chopped
salt and pepper
³/₄ stick lightly salted butter
¹/₂ tsp mace
¹/₂ tsp cayenne
¹/₂ tsp nutmeg
ground pepper

Plunge the shrimp into boiling water to which you have added the shallot, bay leaf, thyme, celery, salt and pepper and cook at full boil for 5 minutes. Drain and toss shrimp in iced water. Peel and press into small ramekin dishes standing in hot water. Melt butter and season with the mace, cayenne, nutmeg and ground pepper. Pour over the shrimp to cover. Cool. Serve with a fresh green salad.

Moules Marinière

This is one of the great dishes from the Atlantic coast of France, where it appears on nearly every restaurant menu. On the west coast of Ireland, it is a regular "free" meal when we go to the rocks at low tide to collect the mussels hidden under curtains of slippery seaweed. It can make a light starter course or a main meal.

4 lb mussels, cleaned, scrubbed, and bearded
¹/₂ stick butter
2 shallots, finely chopped
1 stalk of celery, chopped
1 tsp thyme, chopped
1 bay leaf
pinch of ground pepper
1 wine glass white wine

Clean and beard the mussels under running water, discarding any that are open or seem unduly heavy. In a deep pot, heat the butter and sweat the shallots, celery, thyme, bay leaf and pepper for about 2–3 minutes over low heat. Turn up heat, add a generous glass of wine, and boil a minute or two. Then add the mussels, cover tightly and boil quickly over a high heat for about 2 minutes until the mussels open, shaking the pot a couple of times lightly. Garnish with parsley. Eat with your fingers, using an empty shell to pinch out the mussels, and provide finger bowls. Mop up the juice with lots of crusty bread or provide soup spoons.

Soused Herrings

Maybe it's the line of a song, but it always comes into my head when the subject of herrings comes up: "God bless us and save us" said old Mrs Davis "I never knew herrings was fish". A lovely, delicate, soused herring is a great way to start the day.

4 fresh herrings, filleted
1 medium onion, sliced
2 bay leaves
2 tsp pickling spice
equal parts white malt vinegar and water
salt and pepper

Preheat oven to 300°F. Rub the herring fillets with salt all over. Put them in an ovenproof dish and add the onion, pickling spice, and bay leaves and cover with the malt vinegar and water. Cover with aluminum foil and bake approximately 40 minutes. Allow to cool. Serve with brown bread and butter.

Gravlax

One of the great delicacies of Norway, gravlax (literally "grave" salmon) is an ancient method of curing salmon in prerefrigeration days. Some cooks suggest that it is better to deep freeze the salmon for a day before preparation to kill any bacteria.

1 lb tail-end fillet of wild salmon,
with bones removed but with skin intact
1 tbsp sugar
1 tbsp white peppercorns, crushed
1 tbsp coarse sea salt
3 tbsp fresh dill, chopped

Place fillet on a piece of foil, skin side down. Sprinkle with sugar, then layer with peppercorns, sea salt, and finally the chopped dill. Fold the foil like an envelope and leave it in a refrigerator for 48 hours with a weight on top. To serve, scrape off the marinade with a knife and slice thinly, as for smoked salmon, using a straight-edged carving knife, working diagonally with the grain toward the tail. Cubed potatoes, lightly cooked in cream, with the addition of some fresh dill and a dash of lemon juice make a good accompaniment; or serve as for smoked salmon, with brown bread and lemon wedges.

Ceviche

A method of "cold cooking" raw fish in lime or lemon juice, *ceviche* is said to be of Polynesian origin for which the recipe was first written down in the 1930s. It is one that has been adopted enthusiastically in Mexican cuisine, with added ingredients such as hot chillies and peppers to spice it up. It can be made with other fish like sole or mackerel, although "cooking" times are variable. It is best with scallops as it preserves the incomparably delicate taste of the shellfish.

8 large scallops removed from their shells and cleaned
lime or lemon juice to cover
3 tbsp olive oil
salt and pepper
salad greens, such as lettuce, lamb's lettuce, or arigula
chopped herbs such as chives and parsley
or fresh coriander
a few drops of Tabasco sauce (optional)

Slice the scallops into discs and place them in a glass or ceramic bowl in a bath of lime or lemon juice to cover completely. Marinate for 2 hours, turning occasionally. Drain. Mix 1½–2 tablespoons of this juice with the olive oil, season to taste, and add chopped fresh coriander or parsley and chives. Toss the scallops in this mixture and place on a bed of mixed salad greens.

Ray in Black Butter

Black-butter sauce actually dates back to the sixteenth century, and this dish is one of the classics of French cuisine. This recipe, however, has a major difference in that the ray is simmered in the white wine vinegar, without the usual addition of water, which concentrates the taste. You can substitute skate for ray.

2 large ray wings
2 tbsp white wine vinegar
1 clove garlic , crushed
1 onion, finely chopped
¹/₂ stick butter
capers and chopped parsley to garnish
(serves 2)

You need a large and a small frying pan for this dish. First wash the fish and pat dry. In a wide frying pan heat the vinegar, garlic, and onion and add the fish. Cook for 10 minutes over a low heat, turning several times. Remove the fish from the pan, leaving the juices behind. Scrape off the thin covering membrane with a knife and then remove the flesh from each side of the wings and place in a warm dish. In a smaller frying pan heat the butter until it is brown (watch very carefully that it doesn't turn black) and quickly pour over the fish. Now transfer the juices from the first pan to the second, boil rapidly for a few seconds and pour over the fish. Decorate with parsley and capers and serve with fried zucchini or stir-fried broccoli.

Cod Stuffed with Spinach

A hearty, inexpensive family dish that can be prepared quickly. Fresh spinach can be used instead of frozen, but it takes a little longer. Blanch 1 lb fresh, cleaned spinach in boiling water for 3 minutes, drain completely and chop.

1 medium onion
2 stalks of celery
¹/₂ stick butter
2 x 11-oz pkts of frozen spinach, defrosted
4 cod fillets
1 fish-stock cube
³/₄ pt cream
salt and pepper
2–3oz grated Emmenthal cheese

Preheat oven to 350°F. Chop onion and celery finely and fry in butter until onion is transparent. Add spinach, blend with onion and celery and cook for 2 minutes. Place spinach, onion, and celery on the bottom of a wide baking dish with the cod fillets on top. Blend stock with 3 tablespoons boiling water until fully dissolved, then add cream. Pour over dish, season to taste with salt and pepper, and sprinkle grated cheese on top. Bake for 25 minutes.

Seafood Pasta

Seafood goes well with pasta and this dish is a complete meal in itself. Try to time the cooking so that the pasta is ready just before the sauce.

8oz shrimp
1 lb tagliatelle (fresh if possible)
1/4 stick butter
3 tbsp olive oil
1 shallot, finely chopped
2 cloves of garlic, peeled and finely chopped
1/4 pt white wine

3/4 pt cream
2 tbsp thyme, chopped
2 tbsp parsley, chopped
1 tsp salt
8oz scallops, shucked and sliced into coins
1 lb clean mussels, scrubbed and bearded

Plunge the shrimp into boiling salted water for several minutes until cooked. Put them in iced water to cool, then peel and set aside. Prepare boiling salted water (with a little drop of oil) for the pasta, and cook *al dente* while the sauce is in preparation. Heat the butter and olive oil in a large frying pan and sauté the shallots and garlic until soft over a low heat. Add the wine, cream, thyme, parsley, and salt. Boil for 8–10 minutes until it has a thick consistency, then add the sliced scallops and cook for 1 minute. Add the mussels. Cover and cook for 2–3 minutes or until they open. Finally, stir in the shrimp to warm them through. At this stage your pasta should be ready; put it in a large serving dish and pour the whole mixture over it. Serve immediately.

Striped Mullet with Bacon and Sage

This is a recipe from Jane Grigson's *Fish Cookery* which I have made many times. A silvery-scaled fish that somewhat resembles the sea bass, the mullet is an inshore feeder which gets its sustenance from herbs rather than other small fish. The little thumbnail-like scales get all over the place when you remove them, so work over a large piece of newspaper.

3 x 1 lb striped mullet
6 rashers bacon
12 sage leaves
2oz bread crumbs
³/₄ stick butter
4–5 fl oz dry vermouth
salt and pepper
¹/₄ pt cream

Preheat oven to 400°F. Scale and clean the mullet and slash in 4 or 5 places on each side. Chop the bacon and sage leaves finely together. Fill the slashes with a little of this paste. Mix the rest with the bread crumbs, season well, and stuff into the cavities of the fish. Butter a baking dish lavishly and arrange the mullet side by side. Bake for 15 minutes. Pour over the vermouth and return to the oven for another 10–15 minutes until done. Pour the cream over the fish and leave for another 2 minutes in the oven. Serve immediately.

Lobster

For two people, this is the ultimate luxurious, but simple treat, that needs no introduction. Rich and rare.

1 x ³/₄–1 lb lobster
butter
lemon juice
black pepper, ground
(serves 2)

Plunge the live lobster into boiling salted water for 15 minutes. Allow to cool. Remove the claws and flippers. Crack the large claws with a nutcracker to extract the flesh. Using a heavy knife with a sharp point, cut through the entire length of the lobster body and tail. Spread open and remove the meat. The green part is tomalley, or liver, which is edible as is the red part – the coral, or roe. Discard other parts. Clean two sections of the body shell and reserve. Now put the lobster meat back into the shells and paint with melted butter and lemon juice and sprinkle with black pepper. Serve with fresh asparagus. (Some people suggest that a tart orange juice works well with lobster instead of lemon juice; it's a question of taste.)

Dublin Lawyer An often-quoted recipe for lobster from the late Theodora Fitzgibbon, the distinguished Irish food writer.

Remove all meat from the cooked lobster. Cut the meat into chunks, heat some butter until foaming, and gently heat the lobster meat in it. Warm 4 tablespoons whiskey slightly, then pour into the pan and set it alight (stand back!). Remove lobster to a warm serving dish and keep warm. Add 5 tablespoons of cream to the pan, mix with the pan juices and season. Boil hard for a couple of minutes to reduce the sauce by half, stir in the lobster and serve at once in the shells.

Grilled Mackerel with Gooseberry Sauce

If gooseberries are not available for the sauce for this classic dish, use redcurrants but omit the drops of ginger.

4 fresh mackerel fillets
1 lb gooseberries, washed, and trimmed
Parsley butter:
1 stick softened butter
handful of finely chopped parsley
salt and pepper
1 tsp lemon juice

Preheat broiler. Line a wire rack with foil (mackerel is inclined to stick), or butter the broiling pan. Slash the mackerel twice across the skin side and lay them skin-side down. Mix the ingredients for the parsley butter and paint this onto the fish. Broil for about 1–2 minutes, then reduce heat. Baste again with the butter and continue until fish is cooked. Make the sauce by stewing the gooseberries with a little water until they burst. Add a little bit of sugar to taste and push through a sieve, adding, if liked, a few drops of ginger squeezed through a garlic press.

Fish Cakes

This recipe is a good way of using leftovers and one that is popular with children. You could substitute cod or hake for salmon.

¹/₂ lb cooked salmon, boned and flaked
¹/₂ lb potatoes, boiled and mashed
1 tbsp chives, chopped
1 tbsp parsley, chopped
2 beaten eggs
flour seasoned with salt and pepper
2oz bread crumbs
¹/₄ stick butter
salt and freshly ground pepper

Mix the salmon, potatoes, chives, parsley and seasonings and add one beaten egg to bind. Form into cakes or patties about 1-inch thick, roll in flour, dip in beaten egg, shaking off surplus, then coat in bread crumbs. Heat butter in the pan and fry on both sides until golden.

Gambas a la Plancha

This is the quickest and most delicious way to eat Dublin Bay prawns, or large shrimp, cooked the way they do it in Cadiz, in southern Spain in a heavy flat-bottomed skillet.

Salt prawns or shrimp, leaving them whole. Heat the griddle pan or skillet until so hot that a drop of water will sizzle instantly. Then film it with olive oil and quickly fry the prawns for 2 minutes on each side. Serve immediately with lemon wedges, finger bowls, and plenty of chunky fresh white bread. Messy, but worth it.

Oyster Loaf (*La Médiatrice*)

An eighteenth-century English dish, the oyster loaf became popular in New Orleans at the end of the nineteenth century; and it is said to be what unfaithful Creole husbands gave their wives when they wanted to say "sorry". It is also known in Louisiana as an Oyster "Po' Boy".

1 loaf of French bread, or baguette, cut in half
¹/₄ stick butter
24 small oysters, shucked and drained
cornstarch
2 tbsp olive oil
shredded lettuce
mayonnaise, preferably homemade

Preheat oven to 425°F. Scoop out the bread from the bottom part of the loaf, brush both halves with melted butter and bake for about 15–20 minutes until brown. (Alternatively, you could put them under a hot broiler.) Dip the drained oysters in cornstarch and fry in hot olive oil for about 2¹/₂ minutes. Drain on kitchen paper. Fill the hollowed-out bread shell with the oysters, top with some shredded lettuce and mayonnaise, then close with the other half. Serve in hot slices with guacamole sauce and cold beer.

Pan-Fried Tuna with Fresh Herbs

To anyone who has only ever experienced canned tuna, the taste of the fresh fish, which is more like a meat both in color and texture, comes as an agreeable surprise. This is a fast dish, full of flavor. The herbs, which add fragrance to the oil, can be varied according to season.

1½ lbs tuna fillets (preferably bonito)
¼ stick butter
4 tbsp olive oil
2 cloves of garlic, crushed
3 tbsp fresh chopped herbs, such as winter savory,
rosemary, thyme
parsley and/or lemon balm to garnish

Slice the fillets very thinly (to approx. ⅛ inch). In a bowl add 2 tablespoons of olive oil to the garlic and coat the fillets with it. Heat the remaining olive oil and the butter in a large frying pan and toss in the chopped herbs, sautéing lightly for 1 minute. Turn up heat, add fillets, and fry for approximately 3 minutes, turning them gently from time to time. Serve with pan juices and sprinkle with chopped fresh herbs, such as lemon balm or parsley. Pan-fried potatoes and zucchini accompany this dish well.

Plaice à la Meunière

This was a regular Friday dish when I was growing up and the fish was sold fresh from a delivery van that toured the neighborhood in the mornings. It is quick, though tricky, and it is imperative that the fish be absolutely fresh. You can substitute flounder or sole fillets.

3 plaice, flounder or sole fillets
flour, seasoned with salt and pepper
2 tbsp clarified butter for frying (see below)
¹/₄ stick butter
lemon juice
chopped parsley
(serves 2)

Dust the fillets with seasoned flour. Heat the clarified butter in a frying pan, then quickly fry the fish on each side until it is nicely browned. Transfer fish to warmed plates. Pour off excess butter from pan, give it a quick wipe with towelling paper, then add the fresh (unclarified) butter and heat until brown but not black. You must watch carefully at this point. Quickly add lemon juice and pour over the plaice. Garnish with chopped fresh parsley. Serve with mashed potatoes and spinach.

Clarified Butter Heat 8 ounces of butter and simmer gently until all the moisture has evaporated; this can take up to 30 minutes. When the foam has become brown and crusty, poke it aside with a spoon and strain the butter carefully through muslin or a metal coffee filter into a

wide-brimmed container (not plastic). Refrigerate and cover. It will keep for weeks. Makes approx. ¹/₃ pint.

Salmon en Papillote

A perfect dinner-party dish that can be made with either steaks or fillets of salmon. Its success lies in the succulence of the fish derived from the conserving juices and the array of colors from the surrounding vegetables.

olive oil
1 leek, thinly sliced
(the white part)
4 salmon steaks or fillets
¹/₄ stick butter
12 cherry tomatoes,
cut in half
sliced julienne strips of
green, red and
yellow peppers
juice of 1 lemon
1 wine glass of Noilly Prat
/dry white wine vermouth
salt and pepper
parsley

Preheat oven to 400–450°F. Cut heavy foil into four 12 in x 12 in pieces. Brush each with a tablespoon of olive oil and layer with a bed of leeks. Lay the salmon on the leeks and put a knob of butter on top. Arrange the tomatoes and strips of peppers around the salmon and add lemon juice, vermouth and season with salt and pepper. Scatter with parsley. Fold up the foil tightly at the edges leaving plenty of space and bake on a baking sheet for 15 minutes. Serve with wild rice or new potatoes and snow peas.

Monkfish with Curry, Lemon, and Ginger Sauce

The sweet, succulent, dense flesh of the monkfish has often been called the poor man's lobster. Like its majestic crustacean colleague, it feeds on shellfish. Its terrifying-looking, grotesque head belies a sublime-tasting flesh. It has to be carefully cooked, as it toughens if overcooked. It also makes an ideal fish for kebabs.

2 lb monkfish fillets, thinly sliced	lemon juice
olive oil	1 tsp curry paste
1 clove of garlic, crushed	2 bay leaves
sliced peeled ginger	pinch turmeric
³⁄₄ pt fish stock	³⁄₄ pt cream
1 wine glass dry vermouth	ground white pepper
	salt

Cut fillets into pieces and leave to marinate in a mixture of 2 tablespoons olive oil, garlic, and a few slices of fresh ginger. Heat a thin film of olive oil in a frying pan and add the monkfish, frying lightly for about 20 seconds to seal. Drain off excess oil, add fish stock, vermouth, lemon juice (to taste), curry paste, bay leaves, and turmeric and poach for 2–3 minutes. Remove the monkfish with a slotted spoon, place on a warm dish. Add cream and boil sauce rapidly for 3–4 minutes, until it is of coating consistency. Season to taste. Serve with mashed potatoes studded with chopped fresh chives.

Prawns in Garlic Butter

One of the best seafood restaurants in Ireland, Ahern's of Youghal in Co. Cork has featured this dish on its menu for over 20 years, and it never loses its popularity. It can be served either as a first course with 6 prawns per person or 12 for a main course. Cholesterol watchers, beware; this is a sinful pleasure.

24 large raw Dublin Bay prawns (or large shrimp)
salt
fresh bread crumbs
4 sticks softened butter (you may have some left over)
2 small garlic bulbs, the cloves peeled and crushed
$1/4$ pt red wine
2 tbsp mixed fresh herbs, chopped
freshly ground pepper
1 onion, finely diced

Preheat oven to 400°F. Place the prawns in a large saucepan of boiling salted water. When they float to the top in a couple of minutes, remove and place in iced water. Shell when cool. Blend the butter, garlic, red wine, herbs, pepper, and onion in a blender or food processor. Place a little of this mixture in each hole of an escargot or small ovenproof dish and put a prawn on top. Cover the prawns with more butter and sprinkle bread crumbs on top. Place the escargot dishes in the oven for approximately 10–15 minutes. Serve hot with garlic bread.

Fish Pie with Parsley and Potatoes

An inexpensive, nutritious family dish that needs no accompaniment; this fish pie can be prepared in advance.

1 pt milk
4 cod or haddock cutlets or fillets (about 1¹/₂ lb)
¹/₂ stick butter
1¹/₂ oz flour
1 shallot, chopped
salt, pepper
juice of 1 lemon
good fistful of chopped fresh parsley
8 medium-size potatoes, cooked and mashed

Preheat oven to 400°F. Heat the milk gently in a saucepan and season. Add the fish and poach gently for about 5 minutes until the flesh comes off the bone easily. Strain and reserve liquid. To make the *roux*: heat the butter in a saucepan, then add chopped shallot and fry lightly. Add the flour and the strained milk slowly and stir until it thickens, about 5 minutes. Then toss in the parsley, cook gently for a further 2 minutes, adding the fish, salt, and pepper to taste and finally the lemon juice. Put the mixture in a pie dish and top with cooked, mashed potatoes, to which a little milk and butter have been added. Dot top with a little butter and bake for about 20 minutes.

Goujons of Halibut with Turnip, Orange, and Basil

An elegant, colorful dish that is light and fat free, created by Anton Mosimann. In the eighteenth century, oranges were used to flavor fish as lemons are today.

*1¹/₂ lb halibut fillets, skinned, boned and cut into
goujons (or fingers) of about ¹/₂ oz each
salt and freshly ground pepper
¹/₂ tsp orange peel, finely chopped and blanched
5 fl oz fish stock
³/₄ oz shallot, finely chopped
3 ¹/₂ oz peeled turnips, cut into strips and blanched
8 basil leaves, torn into strips
12 orange segments*

Season the fillets of halibut with salt, pepper, and orange peel. Put the fish stock and shallots into a casserole, add the halibut, cover and poach gently on top of the stove for about 2 minutes. Remove the fish with a slotted spoon and keep warm. Boil the stock and reduce by ¹/₃. Add the turnips and basil and season to taste. Simmer for about 30 seconds; the turnips should be crunchy. Take a little stock out of the pan and place in a small separate pan. Warm the peeled orange segments in this. To serve, place the *goujons* in a suitable serving dish with the turnips and basil and cover with the well-seasoned stock.

Fish and Chip Salad

This original recipe is the brainchild of a Michelin star chef, Paul Rankin of Northern Ireland, who trained in London with the Roux brothers, then ran an hotel in the Nappa Valley in California, and now has his own restaurant, Roscoff, back in Belfast. For this starting course he combines an old favorite, fish and chips, with salad leaves, and a tangy dressing.

1 lb fresh snapper fillets
(or haddock)
mixed salad leaves, such
as lollo rosso, arugula,
or iceberg
2 large baking
potatoes 12–14oz
4 tbsp light olive oil

3 tbsp lemon juice or
wine vinegar
1 tbsp Dijon mustard
1 tsp crushed garlic
vegetable oil for
deep frying
olive oil for frying fish

First peel potatoes and cut into $1/4$-inch-thick chips. Heat the vegetable oil in a deep saucepan until hot, but not boiling, and blanch the chips for 3–4 minutes. Drain the chips and reserve. Blend the light olive oil, lemon juice, mustard, and garlic in a blender or food processor. Heat the vegetable oil again until boiling and deep fry the chips until golden (this happens very quickly). Drain. Heat a little olive oil in a large, heavy frying pan until hot and smoking. Add the fillets carefully and sear them for approximately $1^1/2$ minutes on each side until they have a good color. Remove from heat. Arrange the salad leaves and the chips on a warm plate, add the fillets. Pour the

sauce from the blender into the hot pan, shake once, and toss over the fish. Serve immediately.

How to Broil a Whole Fish

Clean and gut fish, but leave on the head. Leave on the scales if you want to eat the fish off the skin, remove scales (with the blunt edge of a knife by pushing backwards against them) if you want to eat the skin. Fish should be at room temperature before cooking starts. A charcoal fire should be grey and very hot. For medium to large fish (2–3 lb) make a few diagonal slashes on each side for faster cooking. Mix in a cup of marinade of 2 tablespoons olive oil and 1 tablespoon lemon juice, salt, and pepper, with chopped fresh herbs such as thyme, dill, and fennel (whatever is fresh and to hand). Paint this on the fish inside and out and place some extra herbs in the cavity. Use an oiled doubled-hinged wire rack for large and small fish to enable you to turn the fish without touching it.

The oilier the fish, the longer it takes to cook, but in general with fish 6–8 inches from the fire, small fish take 6–7 minutes, medium fish 8–12 minutes, but add 2–3 minutes if it's an oily fish. Large fish can take up to 30–45 minutes depending on oiliness. Keep basting throughout (if you put a spray of thyme in the marinade, it can be used like a brush) and sprinkle salt and pepper on each side of the fish when it is done. For fish kebabs, marinate the fish pieces for about 2 hours before cooking. Allow about 8–10 minutes for cooking. For steaks, such as swordfish, marinate for 2 hours, and add aromatic herbs to the fire (e.g. rosemary); grill, basting, for 20 minutes.

Index